first edition

SAVE SI OBI

FELICIA GUY-LYNCH

ISBN-13: 9780987969385

dedication

TO ALL THOSE STRIVING
TO MAINTAIN SALVATION

There are many
benefits to abstinence

If you can, pay off
your debt. Seriously.

Listen to instrumentals

Be careful when doing
business with friends

Should marriage licences
have an expiry date?

There's a difference
between
self-love & selfishness

Invest in
precious metals

Check your interest rate

Listen

Track your net worth

Find a support team

Set a budget. Period.

Unplug from time to time

Save as much as you can

.

Seek out the
counsel of elders

Treat yourself

Love them like you'll
never see them again

When negotiating a
salary, get the company
to name figures first

Ask relevant questions

Take advantage of EI
(Employment Insurance)

Tell them why you
love them

You ever consider
apprenticeship?

Don't be fake deep

Proceed with caution
when cosigning a loan

Don't flex with
OSAP money

Write notes

Take advantage of
Repayment Assistance

Be persistent
but don't force it

Spend on experiences,
not things

Free up

Say sorry when you
actually mean it

Shop solo

Compliment them.
Genuinely.

Be careful with
Overdraft Protection

Go on a walk together
somewhere beautiful

Save for your
education & retirement

Cook for them

When you get a raise,
increase your savings

Make them laugh

Check your
Equifax credit score

Be spontaneous

Check your
Transunion credit score

KOD: Kill Our Demons

Get a free
chequing account

Family isn't
always blood

Support local
entrepreneurs

Replace carbonated
beverages with
coconut water

Get life, disability &
critical insurance

Cry

Invest in
segregated funds

Emotional intelligence
is cool

Learn how to file your
personal income tax

www.ingramcontent.com/pod-product-compliance
Lightning Source LLC
Chambersburg PA
CBHW021934040426
42448CB00008B/1067